Coping with Divorce?

YOUR PARENTS ARE SPLITTING UP.
YOU SAY YOU'RE HANDLING IT FINE. BUT ARE YOU?

Do you:

1 blame yourself for the divorce?

2 try hard not to show your anger, sadness, or other emotions?

3 find it tough to eat, sleep, or concentrate normally?

4 no longer care about school, friends, or activities that once mattered?

5 feel like there's no one you can turn to?

If you answered "yes" to any of these questions, chances are everything isn't fine. And that's not surprising. Dealing with divorce isn't easy. But in this book you'll find some great strategies to help you learn to cope.

Photographs © 2007: age fotostock: 72 (Esbin-Anderson), 2 (Darren
Greenwood/Design Pics), 59 (Hemera); Corbis Images: 23 (Leland
Bobbé), 43 (Bohemian Nomad Picturemakers), 54 top (Gareth
Brown), 95 (DiMaggio/Kalish), 52 (Randy Faris), 55 bottom (Grace/
zefa), 6, 98 (Ole Graf/zefa), 27 (Matthias Kulka), 79 (Lawrence
Manning), 40 (Simon Marcus), 54 bottom (Robert Recker/zefa), 82
(Royalty-Free), 18 (Chuck Savage), 51 (Michael S. Yamashita); Ellen
B. Senisi: 20; Getty Images: 101 (Altendro Images), 84 (Gabriela
Hasbun/The Image Bank), 77 (Noel Hendrickson/Digital Vision),
102 (Manchan/Photodisc Red), 55 top (M. Nader/Taxi), 89 (Nicolas
Russell/Photographer's Choice), 5 bottom, 11 (Stockdisc); JupiterIm-
ages: 32 (Eric Audras/PhotoAlto), 4, 17, 37, 60 (Bananastock), 69
(Burke/Triolo Productions/Brand X), 70 (Plush Studios/Blend Images),
53 (Thinkstock Images); Monty Stilson: cover; Photo Researchers,
NY/Oscar Burriel: 5 top, 76; PhotoEdit: 14, 15 (Michael Newman), 28
(David Young-Wolff); Robertstock.com/Willie Hill Jr./Camerique Inc.:
103; TIPS Images/ImageState: 62.

Cover design: Marie O'Neill
Book production: The Design Lab

Library of Congress Cataloging-in-Publication Data
Trueit, Trudi Strain.
  Surviving divorce : teens talk about what hurts and what helps / Trudi
Strain Trueit.—1st ed.
    p. cm.— (Choices)
  Includes bibliographical references and index.
  ISBN-10: 0-531-12368-5   (lib. bdg)   0-531-16726-7   (pbk.)
  ISBN-13: 978-0-531-12368-3   (lib.bdg.)   978-0-531-16726-7   (pbk.)
  1. Divorce—Juvenile literature. 2. Broken homes—Juvenile
literature. 3. Children of divorced parents—Psychology—Juvenile
literature. I. Title. II. Series: Choices (Scholastic Inc.)
HQ814.T777 2006
306.89—dc22   2004018423

1 2 3 4 5 6 7 8 9 10 R 16 15 14 13 12 11 10 09 08 07

For every heart that's mending

SCHOLASTIC
CHOICES

Teens talk
about what
hurts and
what helps surviving
divorce

Trudi Strain Trueit

Franklin Watts®

A DIVISION OF SCHOLASTIC INC.
NEW YORK • TORONTO • LONDON • AUCKLAND • SYDNEY
MEXICO CITY • NEW DELHI • HONG KONG
DANBURY, CONNECTICUT

a family shattered

Kristin, 15

a family shattered

"IT WAS OBVIOUS SOMETHING WAS WRONG."

Kristin's Story

One October day, Kristin, 15, came home from school to find her father's car in their driveway. The trunk was open, and a suitcase was inside. Her dad was coming out of the house, carrying an armload of CDs. "He told me to go inside and he would be in to explain," Kristin recalls. "I got scared." She rushed upstairs to her older sister's bedroom. Together, the girls watched out the window as their father packed his car.

Soon, Kristin's dad called her and her 13-year-old brother, Jamie, who was alone in his room, to come downstairs. He told his two youngest children that their mother and he were separating. "He hugged us and said he would see us later because he wanted to be gone before my mother got home," says Kristin. "My dad drove off without even saying goodbye to my sister."

did you know?

Studies have found that young people may suffer emotionally, academically, and socially almost a year *prior* to their parents' break-up—test scores drop, behavioral problems increase, and self-image can plummet.

Divorce Odds

About **half** of all American children **will go through a divorce** in their family, and half of those will have to deal with the collapse of a parent's second marriage.

25%	**25%**	**50%**
of parents have divorced once	of parents have divorced twice	of parents have never divorced

Source: www.divorcereform.com

Kristin was upset but not surprised. "My parents never got along for as long as I can remember. Also, my dad's an alcoholic, and he would spend his whole paycheck on beer and such." A few weeks after Kristin's father moved out, her mother told him over the phone she wanted a **divorce**, a legal judgment to end their marriage. "I was next to my mom when she was telling him," remembers Kristin. "He was saying mean things, which made her cry. I cried, too."

The Good, the Bad, and the Ugly

Half of the adults responding to an online poll conducted by www.DivorceMagazine.com described their divorce as "ugly." Around 38 percent felt their divorce went "okay," and only 12 percent categorized their split as "friendly."

12%
FRIENDLY DIVORCE

38%
OKAY DIVORCE

50%
UGLY DIVORCE

Source: www.divorcereform.com

Untying the Knot

Every year, more than one million American children and teens hear the news that their parents are divorcing. The U.S. Census Bureau found that people marrying for the first time face a 40 to 50 percent chance of getting a divorce in their lifetimes. The odds are even worse for remarriages. Those who walk down the aisle a second time have a 60 percent chance of splitting up. With these kinds of statistics, chances are good that you or someone you know will be touched by divorce.

For Kristin, her parents' divorce came as "a sad relief." She had witnessed their stormy marriage, had felt the brunt of her father's alcoholism through verbal abuse. "Before my dad moved out, it felt like I was walking on a volcano that could explode at any minute. At least now, we have some peace," she says.

When You Get the Bad News:

1 Try not to jump to conclusions or be quick to judge one or both parents.

2 Don't feel guilty. The divorce wasn't your fault.

43% of marriages end in divorce.

Within fifteen years of saying their "I do's," forty-three percent of married couples in the United States say "I don't" and divorce.

Source: The National Center For Health Statistics

3 It's all right to feel shocked, angry, scared, sad, rejected, and confused.

4 Give yourself time to process everything.

5 If it helps, talk to someone you trust about what you're going through.

Derailed by Divorce

"Although I felt the divorce was a good choice and I thought I was happier," says Kristin, "I'm having a hard time at school. I used to be an A+ student, but now I'm failing three classes. I guess you can be sad without realizing it."

20+% of young people have parents who argue excessively prior to their divorce.

Bitter Battles

Research shows more than 20 percent of young people have parents who argue excessively prior to their divorce. Sometimes, the split helps calm these tensions. Other times, the fighting continues after the divorce, with children getting caught in the crossfire. Fortunately, the vast majority of parents do stop battling each other, though it usually takes two to three years after the divorce for things to settle down.

Source: Joan B. Kelly and Robert E. Emery, "Children's Adjustment Following Divorce: Risk and Resilience Perspectives," Family Relations 52, no. 4 (2003): 352–362

Are you grumpy with friends? Struggling to focus in class? If so, your troubles could be stemming from the divorce. "People only have so much emotional and physical energy, and it takes a huge amount of energy to deal with divorce," explains school counselor Betty McCadden. "If you're spending most of your energy worrying about the divorce, you won't have much left for the other things in your life, like schoolwork, friends, and activities."

What to Do?

1 Talk to your school counselor or a favorite teacher about what's going on in your life, and let him or her help.

2 Tell your close friends what's going on. Allow them to support you, too.

3 Give your energy reserves some time to recharge.

4 Recognize that it's going to take a while for you to physically and mentally bounce back.

McCadden says many students don't realize that falling grades, depression, inattentiveness, and behavioral problems in the classroom can be reactions to the divorce. "Kids, and their parents, too, don't draw the connection between what's going on at school and what's going on at home," she says. "They think they are 'lazy' or not trying hard enough, which isn't the case." McCadden says that frequently teens don't come to see her until things have reached a crisis point. Maybe they've failed a class or gotten into a fight at school.

The Positive Side

Kristin, a high school sophomore, was old enough to recognize that her dad's alcoholism had seriously injured her family. She says that knowledge, along with her upbeat personality, made it a bit easier for her to accept things. Also, she was able to release the "pent-up feelings I needed to get out of my system" through talking with her mom and through dancing, an activity she loves.

The Negative Side

Jamie knew his parents fought, but he did not recognize the serious nature of his father's drinking or their financial difficulties. He took his parents split hard. Jamie lost interest in friends and his usual activities, preferring instead to lie in bed and watch television. "He withdrew from us 24/7," recalls Kristin. "It was as if he was trying to block all of us out of his life."

Kristin credits her mother, a social worker, for helping Jamie come to terms with the divorce. "My mom handled my brother really well. She promised him that if he had any questions about what was happening, she would tell him the truth." Jamie was also encouraged to express his emotions in positive ways, such as writing and talking to a mental health **therapist**, a trained counselor who helps people work through their problems.

"My mom handled my brother really well. She promised him that . . . she would tell him the truth."

Gradually, over the next few months, Jamie's gloomy mood lifted. He stopped watching television all the time. He began calling his friends, rejoined his basketball team, and was able to focus on schoolwork once more. Today, Kristin reports that her brother is doing better, though he still struggles now and then. She admits Jamie isn't the only one adjusting. "My parents haven't stopped fighting, only now it's over stuff like **child support**. Divorce has taught me you shouldn't take anything for granted. Not money or people," says Kristin with a sigh, "or love."

Source: U.S. Census Bureau

One out of every **five** American adults **alive today have been divorced at least once.**

Jamie Was Here

"Divorce stinks. Not having my dad around is tough,

even though when he lived with us, he'd yell at us a lot.

I wish he'd get his act together, but I know he won't.

None of us asked for this. If you care about your kids,

why would you treat them like dirt? Why would you

leave and not give them enough money to get by? My

dad would rather get revenge on my mom than take care

of us. It's a selfish attitude. Who's the grown-up here?"

Your Life, Your Story

Everyone comes to terms with divorce differently. How you react will be influenced by such things as the amount of conflict going on between your mom and dad, how much your parents communicate with you, the strength of your support system (the people around you), and whether you are encouraged to share your feelings. It also depends on you: how you choose to relate to your parents, your ease at adapting to change, your ability to express yourself, and your overall personality. A divorce will likely be one of the most stressful events you will ever go through. But you are not alone. Millions of teens have paddled the perilous waters of divorce and survived. You can, too.

Nobody's listening

Pretends everything's fine

Blames himself

Major custody battle

Hasn't eaten today

Dad calls every day

Retreating into herself

Got detention again

Can tell parents anything

Just opened up to school counselor

The Toughest Game of All

Tracy McGrady and Dwyane Wade are star players in the National Basketball Association. Both score more than 20 points per game for their respective teams and have led those squads to playoff appearances. But life wasn't always so blissful for Tracy, a 27-year-old swingman for the Houston Rockets, and Dwyane, a 24-year-old guard for the Miami Heat. Both grew up in single-parent homes. Tracy's mother and grandmother raised him. "Living in a single-parent home is really difficult," Tracy admits. "My parents were never married, so I know what that feels like. It was tough, but my mom and grandma did everything in their power to make me respect both my parents." Accepting parents for who they are really helps ease the pain their breakup causes. That's what Dwyane Wade did. "The way you cope is by loving both parents," he says. "That may be hard to do, but you just love them for bringing you into this world, and you try to be the best you can for both parents."

> "My parents were never married, so I know what that feels like. It was tough, but my mom and grandma did everything in their power to make me respect both my parents."

Source: Sean Price, "Divorce Pains," Scholastic Choices 21, no. 3 (November–December 2005): 6–9

chapter two

Ethan, 15

coming
undone

coming undone

THINGS WERE NOT "PERFECTLY OKAY" AFTER ALL.

Ethan's Story

Ethan never saw his mom and stepdad's split coming. "Everything was perfectly okay," insists the high school freshman. "My stepdad used to bring flowers for my mom. They went out to dinner with friends a lot. Sure, they argued now and then, but everybody fights." Ethan can't help but wonder, Where did things go wrong?

A marriage involves many personal issues. Often, problems are not revealed because they are too private to share or parents want to protect their children. Also, when there are early warning signs, like intense arguments or one parent avoiding the other, a teen may be so accustomed to it that he or she doesn't realize where things are headed. Sometimes, a young person may not want to acknowledge the problem. As he retraced the recent past, Ethan saw that his parents' arguments had increased over the last several months. Things were not "perfectly okay" after all.

WARNING
SIGNS of a marriage in trouble:

1 **Frequent and/or intense arguing**

2 **Physical and/or verbal abuse**

3 **The silent treatment**

4 **Leading separate lives**

Eighty-one percent of married couples in the United States will celebrate their fifth wedding anniversary. Of those, thirty-three percent will reach the twenty-five year mark. Only six percent will still be married fifty years after taking their vows.

81%
FIFTH
ANNIVERSARY

33%
TWENTY-FIFTH
ANNIVERSARY

6%
FIFTIETH
ANNIVERSARY

Source: U.S. Census Bureau

Can We Talk?

If your parents are divorcing, you probably want to know, How did this happen? There are many reasons why a marriage falls apart, including financial problems, drug or alcohol abuse, infidelity, physical or verbal abuse, overwhelming stress, physical or mental illness, or poor communication. Research reveals the most common reason tends to be a gradual growing apart.

It's natural to want to know why your parents are getting divorced, and it's okay to ask about it. Your mom and dad may openly discuss the issue(s) that fueled their split, or they may prefer to keep that information private. If they don't want to give you the details, don't assume things or start guessing at what happened. "When there are family secrets, as there often are in divorces, parents often choose not to tell all the facts to a child," says psychotherapist Elayne Savage. "All too often, the child 'fills in the blanks,' making up his/her own perception of 'the truth.' This version is frequently nowhere near what really happened."

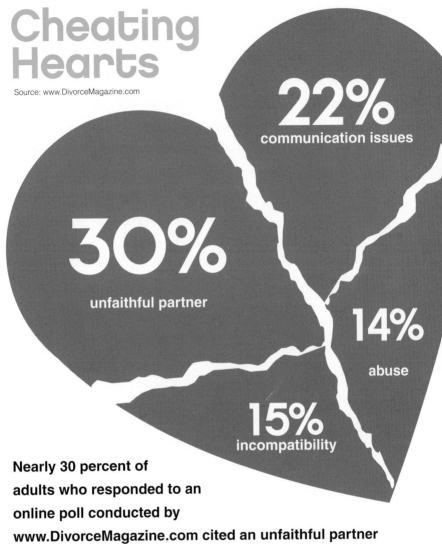

Cheating Hearts

Source: www.DivorceMagazine.com

22%
communication issues

30%
unfaithful partner

14%
abuse

15%
incompatibility

Nearly 30 percent of adults who responded to an online poll conducted by www.DivorceMagazine.com cited an unfaithful partner as the main reason for their separation and/or divorce. Twenty-two percent said communication issues were to blame, followed mainly by basic incompatibility (15 percent) and emotional/physical abuse (14 percent).

With close to half of all American marriages failing, you might be surprised to learn that the United States is not the world's leader in divorces. Belarus, in east-central Europe, is number one on the list, with a 68 percent divorce rate, followed by Russia (65 percent) and Sweden (64 percent). The United States comes in twelfth behind Finland (56 percent) and the United Kingdom (53 percent). Countries with the lowest divorce rates in the world include Italy (12 percent), Turkey (6 percent), and Macedonia (5 percent).

Source: Americans for Divorce Reform

Regardless of the reason(s) behind your parents' divorce, there are two things you can be sure of. First, it is not your fault. Your words or actions did not play a role in the breakup. Divorce is a decision made by a married couple, born from adult issues they weren't able to work out. Secondly, your parents are divorcing one another; they're not divorcing you—even if it feels that way sometimes. For a while, your parents' attention may be focused on adjusting and making arrangements for the future. Your mom or dad may be overly emotional, distracted, irritable, and tired—as may you. A divorce may change the structure of a family, it may challenge the character of a family, but it does not have to destroy a family.

The DURATION of a Marriage

In the United States, first marriages that end in divorce last about eight years. Second marriages don't fair much better, with the median duration being seven years.

Source: U.S. Census Bureau

Bridging the Gap

Trevor remembers his reaction to the divorce: after shock was fear. He "panicked over the little things," like who was going to make his lunch and how he was going to get home after soccer practice. Actually, Trevor's little things were important because they represented his world—a world that had been shaken to its core by divorce. Your parents should answer any questions that you have about the split. They should tell you what is going to happen to you. They should welcome your input as they prepare to make important decisions about your future. However, the reality is that most parents do not do any of these things.

Natalee's Story

"My parents divorced five years ago because my mom is gay. I found out about my mom's sexual orientation about a year before that. She told me she'd been struggling with it her whole life and had started to figure things out after she met other gay women. I respect my mom for making the decision she did. She could have continued in the marriage, but she was true to herself.

"The divorce was an uncomfortable situation for my parents, but they made it as comfortable for us as they could. Both of my parents stayed in the house for more than a year, though my dad moved downstairs. They also waited a couple of years to start dating other people. Most of my friends' parents who are divorcing fight all the time. With my parents, there's no conflict. They were, and are, the best of friends.

"Initially I was embarrassed and upset to tell people that my mom was gay. I was scared that some of my friends would push me away, so I only told a few of them. The struggles that most kids go through with divorce are different from mine. I'm not only adjusting to the divorce, but also to how society judges gays and lesbians.

"Do I feel judged? No. My life is what it is, and my parents are who they are. You hope that people understand, but if they don't, they don't. It's nothing I can control."

Research indicates it isn't common for parents to discuss with their children how the divorce will impact them. In one study, only 5 percent of young people said they had been fully informed about the divorce and were encouraged to ask questions. "Any other family event, like a birth, adoption, or wedding is talked about endlessly, but divorce isn't talked about at all," points out Joan Kelly, noted divorce researcher and psychotherapist. "A significant number of children aren't being told how the divorce is going to affect their lives, and they're very worried."

45%
one- or two-sentence explanation

23%
no explanation

In one study that looked at how divorcing parents communicated with their children, 45 percent of kids said their parents gave them a one- or two-sentence explanation of what was going on, such as "Your dad's leaving." Twenty-three percent of kids said they got no information at all.

Source: Joan B. Kelly and Robert E. Emery, "Children's Adjustment Following Divorce: Risk and Resilience Perspectives," Family Relations 52, no. 4 (2003): 352–362

questions

If your parents are divorcing, you may wonder:

- Whom will I live with?

- How and when will I see the parent I don't live with?

- Will there be enough money to survive?

- Will I have to quit some of my sports and activities?

- Do I have to move?

- Will I be able to see both my parents on birthdays, vacations, and holidays?

Why aren't parents initiating such critical conversations? There are many reasons, say mental health experts, and most are unintentional. A parent may be under the false impression that he or she is protecting you. Sometimes, Mom or Dad doesn't know how to explain things, so nothing at all is said. Other times, a parent is so emotionally and physically exhausted that he or she forgets to keep an open dialogue going. Intense emotions such as anger (at the spouse), sadness, and guilt can also cloud a parent's ability to communicate. Divorcing parents know their actions are hurting their children. By avoiding the topic, they don't have to think about the pain they are causing.

On the flip side, kids may not want to discuss the divorce because "they feel the need to take care of one or both of their parents and don't want to rock the boat any more than it's already rocked," explains psychotherapist Dr. Savage. "Emotions are running high. Kids may fear tears or anger and may try to avoid these emotional displays."

Degrees of Frustration

In an online poll that asked divorced adults how their children were handling the divorce, 31 percent of parents said their kids were "just fine," 33 percent said they were "somewhat upset," and 36 percent said that their children were "quite or extremely upset" by the divorce.

31%	33%	36%
JUST FINE	**SOMEWHAT UPSET**	**EXTREMELY UPSET**

Source: www.DivorceMagazine.com

If it's Tuesday, it must be Dad's house . . . or is it Mom's?

For almost as long as she can remember, Candice Jackson, 15, has led a double life. Splitting time between her parents' homes in neighboring towns, Candy has two houses, two sets of siblings, and two circles of friends. "That's been my life, living out of a suitcase," Candice says. "When I was younger, friends would invite me to sleep over, and I'd have to say, 'No, I'm at my dad's house tonight.' And I could rarely have them over to hang out with me, either. I think what I've missed is the stability." Since she's always kept the lines of communication open with her parents, she still enjoys a loving relationship with both of them. And because she's found ways to speak up, her suitcase life is over. Recently, she moved in permanently with her mom and stepfather. "Divorce is hard, but you can get through it," Candice says. "Now, I cannot even imagine my parents together and still married. But I'm so glad they still talk and work together to help me."

Source: Nancy Fitzgerald and Lisa Jackson, "Dealing with Divorce," Scholastic Choices 18, no. 3 (November–December 2002): 6–10

So what can you do to bridge the communication gap? First, write out any questions that are on your mind—everything from "Where will the cat live?" to "Do I have to change schools?" If there are some special issues worrying you, be sure to list them, too. During a divorce, it isn't uncommon to feel caught in the middle, especially if there's a lot of tension and conflict going on between your parents.

Josh is concerned about how his dad quizzes him about his mother's new life each time he comes back from visiting her. Similarly, Lila feels weird when her mother asks her to remind her dad to make his child support payments on time. "If they want to talk about stuff, they shouldn't use me to do it," she says. "I should be neutral territory." You should never feel pressured to spy on a parent, carry messages between parents, or choose one parent over the other. Even though it might be difficult discussing these things with your parents, it's important to resolve them.

"I should be neutral territory."

are you caught in the
middle?

Does one parent (or both):

- ask you to spy on the other parent?
- press you to carry messages (nice or nasty) between them?
- force you to take sides?
- compete for your love by buying you things?
- put you in the position of playing referee between them?
- accuse you of being just like the other parent when he or she gets mad at you?
- ask you to take on adult responsibilities, such as paying bills or parenting your siblings (taking them to the doctor, disciplining them, etc.)?

If you answered yes to any of these questions, it's time to sit down with your parents and tell them you're feeling caught in the middle. Calmly explain that it's hard on you when they do this and work out a plan with them to make changes.

When you're ready, ask your parent to set aside some time to meet with you. You might say, "I know you have a lot on your mind, but I do, too. I need to talk to you about how things will work out for me." When you sit down with your mom or dad, be direct with your questions and concerns (no one can read your mind). If there is an issue you need to discuss, describe how it makes you feel. For instance, you might say, "Mom, when you insult Dad, it hurts me because I love both of you and I want you to get along."

Once you've spoken, give your parent time to respond. Listen carefully, keep an open mind, and above all, be flexible. Changes are coming, and you will have to adjust. Also, be realistic. You may not like some of the answers you hear. Your parents value your input, but in the end, it is their job to make choices for you they feel are in your best interest. You're not always going to agree. That's okay. The point is to keep the lines of communication open so you can continue to ask questions, share your views, and maintain a strong relationship.

If you're having trouble talking to your parent, try writing him or her a letter. Wait a few days before sending it, to be sure it is what you truly want to say (rewrite it if you want). In your letter, ask your mom or dad to write back. Exchanging letters can help you better understand each other's point of view. It also gives you a way to comfort each other as you both work through the pain of divorce.

TIP/ on TALKING with Your PARENTS:

1. Avoid negative phrases that begin "You always do . . ." or "You never do . . . ," which are exaggerations and only tend to make someone defensive.

2. Keep the discussion focused on your situation and away from your parent's personal problems.

3. Really listen to and consider your parent's responses.

4. Instead of instantly reacting, take time to absorb what your parent has to say. You can always talk again later when you've had a chance to think things over.

the course of divorce

Charlie, 15

the course of divorce

"IF I KNEW A LITTLE MORE . . ."

Charlie's Story

Charlie confesses his "stomach is in knots." His parents recently separated, but he isn't quite sure what that involves. Does separation always lead to divorce? Will he have to move? What's the next step? "If I knew a little more about what to expect," he says, "I think some of these knots might disappear."

Charlie is right, says Elyse Jacobs, therapist and program director at Kids' Turn, a California-based educational program designed to help young people cope with divorce. "Becoming informed about how the divorce process works can help to relieve your fear, anxiety, and stress," she explains. "When you get a wider view of what is happening with the divorce, it makes you feel more comfortable. The pain is still going to be there, but knowledge can help you better adjust."

The **LEGAL** Maze

How much do you know about getting a divorce? Take this true/false quiz to find out. The answers appear on page 44.

1 Parents who separate usually get back together.

2 The average divorce takes one year to complete.

10%

of all adults

living in the

United States

are currently

divorced.

Source: U.S. Census Bureau

3 Most divorces end up in an ugly court battle.

4 If we go to court, a judge is going to make me stand up in front of everyone and choose one parent over the other.

5 Custody arrangements are written in stone. If I want more time with my parent, I won't be able to do anything about it.

Choosing a Path

Legally, a divorce is a court judgment that dissolves, or ends, a marriage. But in real-world terms, a divorce is the whole journey people take to achieve that end. As two married people move from living together to separation and on through divorce, they can choose one of several paths. A divorce can be a relatively peaceful quest, an exhausting battle of wills, or anything in between.

The **LEGAL** Maze

QUIZ ANSWERS

False. Statistics show that most couples who separate will get divorced.

True. The average divorce takes one year to complete.

In the United States, divorce laws vary from state to state. However, there are enough similarities for you to get a good idea of what to expect. Typically, a married couple planning to divorce will first separate, or live apart from one another. They may file a **legal separation** agreement with family court. The agreement is a document outlining how they plan to divide bank accounts and belongings, pay bills, set up two households, and care for their children.

False. Only about one in ten divorce cases in the United States will wind up in court.

False. A judge may interview you privately to find out about your lifestyle, activities, and preferences, but this information is sealed by the court. Your parents won't be able to read it.

False. Custody arrangements can be regularly reviewed and updated if necessary. Your input is important. You can and should get more time with a parent if you need it.

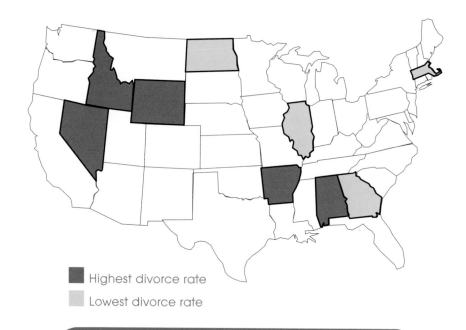

Highest divorce rate

Lowest divorce rate

The Highs and Lows

Nevada has the highest divorce rate in the
United States, which is likely due to the
fact that you don't have to live in the state
to get a divorce there. Arkansas is second,
followed by Wyoming, Alabama, and Idaho.
Massachusetts has, per capita, the fewest
number of divorces, with Georgia, Illinois, and
North Dakota rounding out the bottom group.

Source: National Center for Health Statistics

A couple may also agree on **alimony** and/or child support. Alimony, also called spousal support, is a monthly payment that one partner pays to the other to help that individual maintain a set standard of living. It may go to the stay-at-home mom or dad or to the parent who may be working part-time. It's meant to keep them from sinking into financial straits after the divorce. Child support is money one partner pays to the other to aid in the basic living expenses of their children. It covers a child's necessities, such as food, clothing, housing, education, and medical care.

During a legal separation, a couple is still married. Many states require separation for a set length of time, sort of a cooling-off period, before allowing a divorce to proceed. This gives two people ample time to think about whether they truly want to split up. After being apart for a while, a couple may decide to get back together, but this is unusual. In most instances, separation leads to divorce.

CHILD SUPPORT:

covers a child's necessities, such as food, clothing, housing, education, and medical care.

Money Troubles

About 7 million adults in the United States are due child support—the vast majority of whom are women. Yet, only about 5 million of those who are owed support receive either partial or full payment from their former spouses.

Source: U.S. Census Bureau

Legally Speaking

If a divorcing couple agrees on how to divide **assets** and raise their children, they write up a formal contract. Both people—or parties, as they are legally known—sign the agreement. They, or their attorneys, will file the contract with the court. Frequently, a hearing date is set so that a **family court** judge can make certain the agreement is fair and that the children are emotionally, physically, and financially provided for. Once satisfied, the judge signs a decree of dissolution that legally ends the marriage.

REALITY CHECK:
They're Not Getting Back Together

Alma's parents separated when she was 5, and they later divorced. The end of the marriage didn't surprise her, but that didn't keep her from wishing her parents would get back together. "I was really sad," Alma says. "I kept writing, 'I hate my life' in the sand at my school." She says it took time for her to realize that her parents weren't going to reunite and for her to be okay with that.

The hardest moments for Alma are when she leaves her dad's house after a visit. Her parents live in separate states, and she sees her father mostly on holidays and long weekends. The flights home used to result in crying, and sometimes they still do. "But most of the time, I'm like 'Bye, Dad' because I'm so used to it," Alma says.

She has gotten used to other changes as well, such as her mom and dad dating different people and the idea that each could remarry. Talking to friends has helped her deal with these issues, but the greatest help has been having two parents who get along and pay attention to her needs. "I've survived, and I'm actually living a good life," Alma says.

Source: Sean Price, "Divorce Pains," Scholastic Choices 21, no. 3 (November–December 2005): 6–9

If two people are not able to work out their differences, things get more complicated. Depending on how willing the parties are to cooperate, the following options are open to them:

- **Attorney negotiations:** Each party hires an attorney to look out for his or her best interests. Both sides review bank statements, property lists, and other details. They meet to negotiate a deal.
- **Mediation:** A neutral person, known as a mediator, is hired by the parties to help settle unresolved issues. A mediator is not a judge, but rather a person trained to help others resolve their issues (in most states, mediators do not have to be licensed). Without taking sides, a mediator offers creative suggestions and alternatives for working out problems. The parties do not have to accept anything they don't agree to.
- **Arbitration:** A divorcing couple may choose to give up their decision-making power to an arbitrator. Similar to a mediator, an arbitrator is a neutral third party, perhaps a retired family court judge or attorney. However, unlike a mediator, an arbitrator has the authority to make decisions that are binding, or final. Both parties must accept the arbitrator's ruling.

- **Courtroom trial:** When a couple is unable to settle their disputes in other manners, they may go to court. At trial, both parties and their attorneys appear before a judge to present their arguments. Children are rarely called to testify. The judge examines all documents, listens to both parties and their witnesses, and considers the arguments. In most states, the judge has about ninety days to issue a decision. If either parent is unhappy with the ruling, he or she can file an **appeal** to a higher court.

Between **50–80%** of divorces that go through **mediation** are settled SUCCESSFULLY.

Source: M. Benjamin and H. H. Irving, "Research in Family Mediation, Review and Implications," Mediation Quarterly, 1995, from www.divorceinfo.com

What About You?

One of the biggest decisions facing a divorcing couple is custody, or how to raise and care for their children. Parents must decide two major points: **physical custody** and **legal custody**. Physical custody determines who you will live with once the divorce is final and how much time will be spent with each parent. Legal custody refers to who will handle making important decisions on your behalf in areas such as education, health care, and religious training.

Under each of these custody categories, a parent may either have **sole** or **joint custody**. Sole custody means that one parent is in charge, while joint custody indicates that both parents share in the responsibilities. The parent who has sole custody is called the **custodial parent**. He or she may receive child support payments, either weekly or monthly, from the **noncustodial parent** (the parent who doesn't have custody). Child support is determined by family lifestyle, a child's needs, and parents' income. A regular schedule will be set up to ensure that the child is able to spend time with the parent he or she does not live with.

getting in trouble a lot at school

grumpy with friends

headaches, insomnia, and upset stomach

DIVORCE

losing interest in activities and life

plunging grades

talk to your friends

take time to recharge

talk to a teacher or counselor

- IMPROVEMENT AT SCHOOL
- RENEWED INTEREST IN LIFE
- HEALTHEIR ATTITUDES
- BETTER RELATIONSHIPS

keep your feelings to yourself

pretend things are okay

- LONELINESS
- ISOLATION
- FEAR
- WORRY

what teens
WANT

The most typical custody arrangement in the United States is joint legal custody, where one parent has sole physical custody and the other has visitation rights. Yet, research shows teens frequently prefer joint physical custody and joint legal custody, because they want both parents equally participating in their lives.

JOINT

custody

When divorcing parents agree on custody, they write up a **parenting plan** (often with help from legal counsel) for a judge to finalize. The parenting plan outlines a visitation schedule, settles transportation issues, and may include arrangements regarding holidays, birthdays, and vacations. However, if two people cannot agree on how to raise and support their children, the matter falls to a judge to decide.

For many young people, the main issue isn't whom they live with as much as it is getting adequate time with the parent they don't live with—and that's usually Dad. Of the twenty-one million children in this country living with one parent, about 80 percent are residing with their mothers. Research shows that, generally, children get every other weekend with their noncustodial parent. "What children are telling us is that it's just not enough time," reveals divorce researcher Joan Kelly. "More than half of kids say they want equal time with both parents, but all they are getting is four days a month with the parent they aren't living with. They spend a weekend, then have to wait twelve days to see that parent again, when what they really want is to wait only a day or two."

Balancing Priorities

school
activities
friends
siblings
relationships
with parents
my opinion

work and travel schedule
mental and physical health
ability to nurture
style of discipline
financial
situation
**criminal
history**

**When determining
custody, a judge
weighs your
parent's situation
with your needs
and lifestyle.**

Don't be shy about discussing custody issues with your parents. Speak up if you're not getting enough time with your mom or dad. "What I need," says 16-year-old Emily, "is for both my parents to be in my life as much as possible. I think that's what every kid needs, divorce or no divorce."

What I need

The
TWO-HOME
TEEN

"When I go to my dad's house, I only spend one night,"

says Gabrielle. "I don't feel at home there yet." Adjusting to traveling between two households can be challenging, but there are things you can do to make it easier:

1. Make a checklist of everything you want to take with you to your noncustodial parent's place. Laminate it and keep one copy at your mom's and another at your dad's.

2. Design an in/out basket for each home. This is the place where you'll keep homework and other items that go back and forth with you.

3. Ask if you can keep some of your own stuff at your noncustodial parent's house, like video games, DVDs, makeup, jewelry, and clothes. If it's okay, decorate your room.

chapter four

Paige, 16

sea of
emotions

sea of emotions

"YOU LOSE TOUCH WITH YOUR REAL SELF."

Paige's Story

"I was all over the place emotionally," says Paige, 16, remembering how she felt when her parents told her they were divorcing. "One day I'd be praying for them to get back together, and the next I'd be furious at their arguing. You lose touch with your real self in all the chaos."

Dealing with the turmoil of divorce may mean confronting intense and ever-changing emotions. More conflict between parents usually means more emotional distress for you. Toss in the usual pressures that come with schoolwork, friendships, dating, and body image, and it isn't hard to see why teens trying to handle their parents' breakup may feel overwhelmed.

EMOTIONAL

HIGHƧ
lows

contentment
acceptance
hope

bitterness
confusion
loneliness

Do you feel like you're trapped on an emotional roller coaster? Experts say it's normal to go through highs and lows as you adjust to the changes divorce brings. In the meantime, talk to someone you trust when things get rough. This is one ride you don't have to take by yourself.

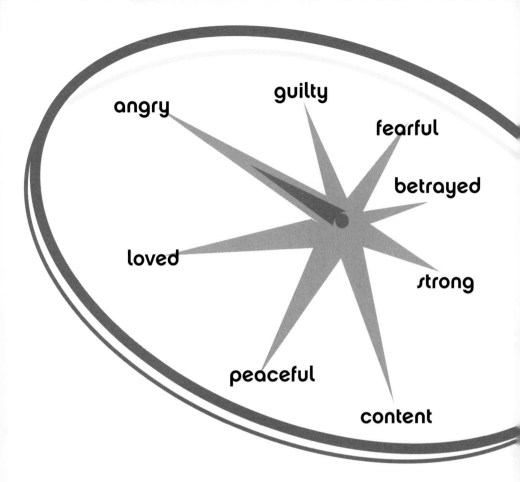

Where Is Your Emotional Compass Pointing?

On paper, draw a compass and point the needle at whatever emotion is currently the most powerful in your life. Expand on these emotions to create your own list, if you like. Do this exercise whenever you're feeling uncertain and want to gauge your state of mind.

Good Grief

Whenever something ends, whether it is friendship or the life of a loved one, part of coming to terms with it involves expressing sorrow, or grieving. Unfortunately, a divorce, too, reflects loss: the loss of living together as a family, loss of freedom as you juggle a new schedule, or perhaps the loss of your childhood if you're looking after siblings or comforting a devastated parent. Experts have broken down the grief process into five stages:

- denial
- anger
- bargaining
- sadness
- acceptance

There is no right or wrong way to grieve. Everyone copes with loss differently. You may find you stay in one stage longer than the others, skip a stage, or go back and repeat a stage. Also, there is no time limit on grief. It takes as long as it takes for you to heal.

Grieving Divorce Timeline

Your grief experience won't be like anyone else's. You may remain in one stage longer than another, skip a stage completely, or go back and repeat a stage. There is no time limit for grieving your parents' divorce. It takes as long as it takes.

SOURCE: DIVORCE MAGAZINE at www.DivorceMagazine.com

Denial

A refusal or inability to acknowledge the divorce. In this stage, a teen believes his/her parents will reconcile and may contrive to make that happen.

Anger

Borne out of the inability to control the situation, anger is directed at one or both parents, siblings, teachers, the world, or even oneself.

Bargaining

Feeling helpless or that he/she did something to cause the divorce, a teen may try to bargain to fix things. "If you come home, Dad, I promise to get straight A's."

Sadness

As a teen begins to let go of his/her old life, it's normal to feel blue. However, sadness left to fester for too long may slide into depression, and require professional help.

Acceptance

A coming-to-terms with the divorce. Acceptance doesn't mean forgetting what's happened, rather that denial, anger, bargaining, and/or sadness are no longer used to cope or to try to recover what's been lost.

Sometimes, people deal with loss in unhealthy ways. They may act out, or behave in an inappropriate manner, play the victim, or sink into self-destructive patterns. These behaviors are called defense mechanisms. Relying on these methods to handle problems can trap us. Defense mechanisms keep us from accepting reality, adjusting to change, and moving forward. The rest of this chapter will focus on the emotions young people most often experience in dealing with their parents' breakup. Maybe you can relate to them.

Was It Me? A Guilt Complex

"My parents had a fight about letting me go camping with friends the same night my dad left for good," says Haley, 14. "I figured if I hadn't asked to go on the trip, they never would have argued and my dad wouldn't have walked out. My therapist helped me to see that I had nothing to do with it. Their relationship had been going downhill for a couple of years, ever since my dad had an affair. They had bigger problems than whether I went camping or not. You have to know with divorce, there's usually a lot going on behind the scenes."

Are you playing the blame game? Do you say to yourself, "This divorce would not have happened if only I had done _____ (fill in the blank)" or "if I had not done _____ (fill in the blank)?" If so, you need to recognize that this is an inaccurate way of thinking. Remember, a divorce springs from unresolved adult issues. You did not cause it. You cannot fix it. So stop taking the blame for it.

Turning Back Time

A www.DivorceMagazine.com survey asked readers, "If you could change the past would you still be getting (or have gotten) a divorce?" Eighty percent of women and 58 percent of men who responded answered yes. If they had to do it all over again, they would still choose to get out of their marriage. Source: www.DivorceMagazine.com

Tori's Obsession

Two years after her mom and dad divorced, Tori was still trying to patch up a marriage that no one could persuade her was over. Tori arranged things so her mom and dad would show up at the same time to pick her up from ballet. Once, she pretended to be sick at school and called them both to come and get her. Tori admits she was "obsessed with fixing" her family, thinking that if she could just get her parents together, they would somehow fall in love all over again. It didn't work, of course. You need to know that the decision to divorce is not easily or hastily made. It requires careful thought and is usually undertaken as a last resort, when every other option to save the marriage has failed.

The Boiling Point:
Anger and Betrayal

When Will learned that his mom and dad were separating, he wanted to explode, which is exactly what he did. Will smacked his hand against the kitchen countertop and broke a finger. His outburst was an expression of the betrayal, helplessness, and hurt burning inside. It isn't uncommon for strong feelings of anger to bubble to the surface in response to divorce. You may wonder, How could my parents put their desires ahead of the family? Why didn't they try harder to save the marriage? Doesn't anyone care about what I want? Perhaps the divorce is forcing you to make changes you aren't thrilled about, such as moving to a new neighborhood, cutting corners financially, or traveling back and forth between your parents' homes.

It's healthy to release your anger by talking, exercising, or even punching a pillow (not the countertop). If anger is left to fester, a person may act out by becoming irritable, moody, defensive, or short-tempered. It may involve something small, like snapping at a sibling for no reason, or it may grow into a far more serious problem, such as fighting at school, stealing, or vandalism. Other forms of acting out include defying authority, substance abuse, and engaging in irresponsible sexual activity.

Putting
out the
FIRE

Try these ideas when anger is smoldering within you. Then, when you're calmer, sit down with your parents and talk about what's been fueling your flames.

- Hit a pillow or punching bag.
- Take a walk around the neighborhood.
- Go skateboarding, biking, jogging, or play your favorite sport.
- Get up and sing or dance to music.
- Write in your journal.
- Chat online or on the phone with a friend.

behind the
WALL

"I put up a wall to keep people out," says Marco, describing how he latched on to rage after his parents' divorce. "I was this tough guy who didn't care about anybody or anything. I hurt people first before they had a chance to hurt me. Nobody messed with me at school. Everyone thought I was cool, but really I was scared and miserable."

In a Funk: Sadness and Depression

After her parents separated, Jordyn says she "fell into a kind of depression." Alone in her room, she would curl up with her kitten and listen to music. If you're going through a divorce, it is natural to feel down in the dumps for a short time. Yet, Jordyn's sadness went too far. It began to interfere with her life and her health. "On the inside, I felt horrible," she says. "I changed everything about me: how I looked, dressed, and acted."

Thinking she was overweight, the 117-pound high school freshman went on a drastic diet. She admits she would have done serious harm to herself if her mother hadn't stepped in and gotten her to a therapist. Jordyn is now in recovery for her depression and eating disorder. Now she understands where things went wrong. Because she couldn't control the divorce, she turned to the things she could control: food and her weight.

BEYOND
the BLUES

1. Do activities you once enjoyed no longer bring you happiness?
2. Are you having trouble concentrating at school?
3. Have you noticeably lost or gained weight?
4. Do you sleep too much or, perhaps, too little?
5. Are you plagued by feelings of guilt or hopelessness? Do you feel that your life has no point?

If you answered "yes" to most of the questions above (especially the last one), and you've felt this way for more than a few weeks, YOU NEED TO GET HELP NOW. Talk to your parents, your family doctor, or school counselor right away. You could be suffering from depression, a serious mental disorder that affects nearly three million young Americans. With medical treatment, most people with depression lead normal lives. If you're showing the signs of depression listed above, don't wait for them to go away. Get help now.

Castaway:
Rejection and Abandonment

"My mom and dad kept saying they couldn't get along, they couldn't communicate, but what about me?" wonders Sam. "My dad didn't just leave my mother. He left me, too." During a divorce it's normal to feel rejected, especially by the parent who is moving out. Because his father was no longer living with him, Sam feared his dad would not want to be part of his life. Yet this wasn't true. Indeed, it's rarely the case. After divorce, most parents continue to love, communicate with, support, nurture, and spend as much time as they can with their children.

Sometimes, a parent may not stay in touch as often as he or she desires or should. This is particularly true in cases that involve a parent in prison, heightened conflict, or a parent's moving. When a mother or father disconnects from the child's world, intentionally or unintentionally, it can cut deeply. Feeling abandoned, you might wonder, if the one person that I thought loved me the most has walked out of my life, how important and lovable could I be? Such thoughts can be a devastating blow to your self-esteem, which is a person's belief in his or her own worth as a human being. "Don't buy into your parents' issues and connect them to your own self-worth," warns Abby Peterson, a child and family counselor. "You have to remember the divorce has nothing to do with you." If you are feeling worthless, it's okay to acknowledge such feelings, but don't let them linger and take root.

"You have to remember the divorce has nothing to do with you."

Research reveals that most teens—used to seeing their noncustodial parent every day prior to the divorce—only get about *four days a month* with that parent after the divorce.

Source: Joan B. Kelly and Robert E. Emery, "Children's Adjustment Following Divorce: Risk and Resilience Perspectives," Family Relations 52, no. 4 (2003): 352–362

Less Than ZERO

"I can get really down on myself sometimes," confesses Brooke, whose parents are going through a bitter divorce. "They are always fighting over child support money that my dad owes my mom. When my dad doesn't pay, it's hard on me. I feel like he doesn't want me to live. Otherwise why wouldn't he contribute to making my life a little better?"

The Power Within

Human emotions are a strong force. Your feelings have the ability to affect your thoughts, actions, self-esteem, and even your health. What emotions is the divorce sparking within you? Are you wrapping yourself in a blanket of guilt? Unleashing your fury on loved ones? Retreating into sadness? Think about how you are handling your feelings. Are they impacting your energy level, health, schoolwork, activities, and relationships with others?

The good news is that studies indicate most of these tumultuous emotions you are experiencing will fade within the first year or two after the divorce. Rest assured, in time, you will feel better. Although you didn't choose the divorce, you can choose how you respond to it. You can successfully navigate the emotional storm of divorce. The next chapter will show you how.

What emotions is the divorce sparking within you?

Figures show that about 35 percent of kids have at least weekly contact with their fathers in the first two to three years following the divorce. However, 18 to 25 percent of children have no contact with their fathers two to three years after the divorce.

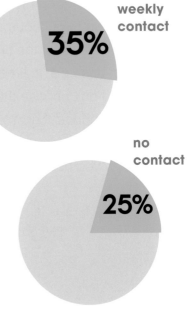

weekly contact

35%

no contact

25%

Source: Joan B. Kelly and Robert E. Emery, "Children's Adjustment Following Divorce: Risk and Resilience Perspectives," Family Relations 52, no. 4 (2003): 352–362

A New Light

One way to prevent divorce from chipping away at your self-esteem is to view the situation from a new angle. Psychotherapist Elayne Savage says to pretend for a moment that you are an onlooker. Ask yourself,

"What's one reason, that doesn't have anything to do with me, why my parent isn't _____ (fill in the blank: visiting, paying support, discussing things with me, etc.)?"

Is he or she far away? A workaholic? Arguing a lot with your custodial parent? When you look at things from a different perspective, you'll begin to see the truth has nothing to do with you.

chapter five

Jaclyn, 18

divorce:
a survival guide

divorce: a survival guide

"I STARTED GETTING MIGRAINES."

Jaclyn's Story

"My parents' separation and selling our house was a nightmare, but I was sure I could handle it," says 18-year-old Jaclyn. "I was so wrong. I started getting migraines. I was under too much stress, you know, taking my SATs, keeping up my grades, and focusing on my sport [Jaclyn is a champion swimmer]. The divorce put me over the edge."

If you're dealing with divorce, no doubt it feels as if your world is crumbling. Can you rebuild your life? Is it possible to have a successful future? Fortunately, the answer to both questions is yes.

First, it's important to acknowledge something that may seem obvious—the divorce has hurt you. Even if you think it was a wise decision for your family, seeing your parents split up is heartbreaking. Second, you need to realize that some things in life, like divorce, are beyond your control. However, there are some things you can take charge of: your thoughts, feelings, and actions. Expressing yourself in a positive manner helps you cope. It allows you to feel better in the short-term and mend in the long term. On the following pages, you'll find some healthy ways to free the emotions that may be churning inside you. Some are as easy as getting up off the couch, while others will challenge you to take a bit of a risk. Ready?

Is Divorce Making You Sick?

Research has found that unexpressed emotions may trigger minor physical ailments, like headaches, stomachaches, or insomnia, which is the inability to fall and stay asleep. Studies show that, over time, pent-up emotions can increase the production of stress hormones and lower the function of the immune system, your body's ability to fight illness and disease.

Take Your First Steps Toward HEALING:

5 Release stress in healthy ways.

4 Start focusing on you.

3 Accept that the divorce is out of your hands.

2 Know that you're going to hurt for some time.

1 Admit the divorce has hurt you.

Work It Out

When you're simmering with fury or frustration, a quick way to vent those feelings is through physical activity. Go for a walk, run, or bike ride. Swimming, skateboarding, soccer, or even dancing around your room are good ways to blow off steam while doing something healthy for your body.

In the long term, building a regular exercise program into your schedule will help to reduce the chance that you'll release feelings in negative ways, such as raiding the refrigerator or blowing your top at a friend. Did you know that when you exercise, your brain releases chemicals, called endorphins, that work naturally to relax you and lift your mood? When you're calmer, you think clearer and are more likely to make better decisions. The U.S. Department of Agriculture (USDA) and other fitness experts recommend healthy teenagers get sixty minutes of physical activity each day. Before beginning any exercise program, consult your doctor to ensure you are in good health and to assist you in selecting the best type of exercise for you.

TIPS

Here are a few tips that will help get you moving for a lifetime.

- Choose an exercise you like.
- Start slowly. Exercise for ten minutes to begin and gradually increase intensity and length of training time as you go.
- Vary your routine.
- Work out with a friend.
- Don't get discouraged. If you miss a few days or even a week, don't quit. Simply recommit yourself and start again.

Source: USDA

Nutrition Matters, Too!

In 2005, the USDA replaced its Food Guide Pyramid with MyPyramid, a program that takes an individualized approach to nutrition and fitness. Go to www.mypyramid.gov to get a customized food plan and activity recommendations targeted to your age, gender, and fitness level.

Talk It Out

"It's important to talk about what you're going through," explains art therapist Elyse Jacobs. "Just saying your feelings out loud to someone gives your emotions a place to go. You realize that a feeling is here and now, but it won't last forever." If you have a parent encouraging you to express your feelings, and you feel comfortable doing so, you are fortunate. Yet many kids feel the way Cara does. "How can you talk to your parents about how much you're hurting when they are the ones hurting you?" she asks. It's okay to discuss the divorce with someone outside of your family who can listen without judgment and offer support. Confide in someone you trust, such as a school counselor, favorite teacher, neighbor, religious leader, or an understanding friend who has been through divorce.

"Just saying your feelings out loud . . ."

You may also want to seek assistance from a licensed mental health professional. It may be a bit scary discussing your personal issues with an adult you don't know, but therapy is a safe harbor in the storm of divorce. A therapist will not discuss anything you say with your parents, and can offer problem-solving strategies you might not have considered. "I'm here to help you and your family through a hard time," emphasizes child and family counselor Abby Peterson, founder of Family Room in Seattle, Washington. "Kids come here to relax and talk, or not talk, if that's what they feel like doing. If you think you have to be the gleaming, happy, shiny kid for the rest of the world, this is the one place where you can drop the good, gleaming, happy, shiny stuff and get ugly."

SHOCK WAVE: Is It Over Yet?

Do you have a strong support system? Still trying to go it alone? To find out, take the following quiz. On a separate sheet of paper, answer each of the questions with "always," "sometimes," or "never." Score 2 points for every "never," 1 point for each "sometimes," and 0 for "always."

1. My parents don't know my friends.
2. If I want something and don't get permission from one parent, I usually get permission from the other.
3. I feel better when I keep my thoughts to myself.
4. I believe neither parent wants me to love the other parent.
5. My parents don't encourage me to talk with an adult I can trust outside of the family.
6. My parents expect me to tell on each other.
7. Nobody wants to hear about what is happening with me.
8. I'm afraid to tell one of my parents something the other parent told me to keep a secret.

Source: Abby E. Peterson, MA, LMHC, www.afamilyroom.com

12 to 16 points: Great job! It sounds like you're doing all right and have a good understanding that things are working out.

7 to 11 points: Things are probably difficult for you to figure out alone. Think of someone you can talk to: a person you can rely on in your support system.

0 to 6 points: Chances are you would benefit from the support of an adult. It's in your best interest to ask for help from someone you can trust, such as your school counselor or a therapist.

Reach Out

High school student Daniela Romano, whose
parents were divorced, was e-mailing a frazzled
friend dealing with divorce when an idea struck her.
Why not start a chat group where teens coping with
divorce could connect with one another? With her
dad, Daniela launched the Kids 4 Kids network in
her New Jersey High school. Two years later, the
Web site www.kids4kids.com was born. The site,
which is sponsored by the nonprofit New Jersey
Council for Children's Rights, gives teens a chance
to share stories, swap advice, and open up about
any divorce topics they choose. The only rule?
No adults allowed. Trained high school volunteers
monitor the chats and assist kids in getting
professional help when necessary.

"Kids of divorce have so much weighing on their minds. This is a place where they can go to vent their feelings without having to worry that their parents will listen in to what they are saying," says Daniela, who knows firsthand the trauma divorce can cause. In 1991, when she was 6 years old, Daniela was snatched by her mother and taken cross-country during a custody fight. It would take her father fifteen months to win custody and bring Daniela home (today, her parents have a healthy post-divorce relationship).

Peer Power

If you're feeling alone, why not join a peer support group for kids of divorce? Usually led by a trained mental health professional, it's a place where you can feel free to talk confidentially without your parents around, exchange ideas, learn the facts about divorce, and make new friends. Many churches, schools, and community centers offer peer support groups. If there isn't one near you, talk to your school counselor about starting one at your school.

My Mom Is Dating Again. Ew.

"I was just getting over the split and now this," groans Katherine, referring to her divorced mother's new boyfriend. *"I'm only starting to date myself. Is my life ever going to be about me and not her?"* After all you have been through with the divorce, it's natural to resent a parent who strikes out to find a new relationship. Still, your parent is a human being who, like you, desires love. Also, the reality is that 75 percent of divorced men and 65 percent of divorced women in the United States will remarry.

If seeing your parent date bothers you, ask yourself why. Are you jealous because a boyfriend or girlfriend is taking your parent's time and attention away from you? Maybe you are worried that someone else may try to replace your mom or dad. Talk to your dating parent about your concerns. If you need some one-on-one time with your parent, set up a regular day and time each week to get together. Also, it's okay to ask your mom or dad about where their new relationship might be headed. Remember, you don't have to like whomever your parent is dating, but be respectful. If you keep in mind that nobody can replace your parent in your heart or in your life, you might one day discover there's enough room in both places for one more person to love: a stepparent.

A Bright Future

In his poem about divorce, "A Cry for Help,"
14-year-old David from Kentucky writes:

> I now understand how terrible and amazing it
>   is at the same time.
> Terrible because your whole world is torn
>   apart.
> Amazing because it makes you even stronger
>   than before.

Worthen, Tom (editor). broken hearts...
healing: young poets speak out on divorce.
Logan, Utah: Poet Tree Press, 2001.

Many young people say going through their
parents' divorce built their character, made them
more resilient, and helped them become more
compassionate toward others. "Before the divorce,
it was all about what I wanted," admits Stephanie.
"Now I feel the need to reach out to others."

"Now I feel the
need to
REACH OUT
to others."

Another benefit of divorce may be a newfound peace. "When parents move on and are happier with their surroundings, kids have the opportunity to find a greater happiness than what they have already known," explains Peterson.

"I don't want my parents back together," says Kristin, whom you met at the beginning of this book. "Divorce itself is a terrible thing, but when you go through it and come out the other side, you realize that the peace you've found is worth all the sorrow."

"... you realize that the peace you've found is worth all the sorrow."

Going through a divorce may:

open up your heart to the suffering of others

make you aware of a support network of friends and family

teach you how to better communicate and express yourself

make you a stronger, more resilient person

give you more quality time with a parent

bring you closer to siblings and relatives

bring more peace to your life

BEFORE
Tying the Knot

Many divorced people recognize too late their mistake of not discussing their desires, goals, and expectations with each other when they were dating. Here are some issues for you to think about and talk about with that special someone, before saying "I do."

1. How many children do you want? Do you even want children?
2. If you have children, should one person be a stay-at-home parent? Which one?
3. Should you pool your finances or have separate bank accounts? Who should pay the bills?
4. What are your career goals?
5. How should household chores be divided?
6. How do you define success? Is it a good job? Material things? Spending time together?
7. What does it mean to be a good husband/wife?

"Divorce teaches you what not to do," says Cody. "I still want to get married someday, but I want to communicate better than my parents did. I want to take my time finding someone special. I don't want the divorce to change me or what I want for my future."

Divorce does not have to alter you or your goals. "Years of research tell us that the majority of kids of divorce go on to lead productive lives," reveals Joan Kelly, noted divorce researcher and psychotherapist. "Yes, they are at greater risk for divorce when they grow up, but most are functioning at an average or better-than-average level."

A long, difficult chapter in your life is closing. But a new one waits to be written. You hold the pen. You can wallow in the pain or let the wounds heal. You can struggle with self-doubts or strengthen your self-esteem. You can choose to be a victim or a survivor. The story is yours to write. Now turn the page. And begin.

Studies reveal that **75 to 80 percent** of kids of divorce grow up to be fairly **well-adjusted**, achieve their academic and career goals, and keep close ties to their families.

Source: Joan B. Kelly and Robert E. Emery, "Children's Adjustment Following Divorce: Risk and Resilience Perspectives," Family Relations 52, no. 4 (2003): 352–362.

Making Peace with the Past

When writer Craig Henry Leibel proposed to his wife, "all of a sudden questions, concerns, and fears rang through me like a bulldozer," he recounts. "It was then I realized how much my parents' divorce was still affecting and controlling the decisions in my life." Determined to escape the shadow of his parents' divorce, Leibel wrote **Within a Child's Heart** *at age twenty-three. The book, which delved into his childhood experience with divorce, helped him come to terms with his past and reach out to others. "As a child of divorce, I believe to conquer and heal from the effects of divorce is not to look for closure or a specific ending with it, but to accept it as part of who you are," he advises.*

alimony—the temporary payment of money by one spouse to another to allow that individual to maintain a certain standard of living

appeal—the legal process by which the losing party in a divorce asks a higher court to review the decision of a lower court

arbitration—a form of dispute resolution conducted by an arbitrator, or neutral third party, whose decisions on the issues are usually legal and final

assets—property of value, such as cash, real estate, investments, jewelry, furniture, artwork, cars, and other similar belongings

child support—money paid by one spouse to the other following a divorce to aid in the living expenses of their children

custodial parent—the parent with whom a child lives after a divorce

divorce—a legal judgment ending a marriage; also called a dissolution

family court—the segment of the legal system designed to handle matters dealing with divorce, such as custody, child support payments, and visitation rights

joint custody—when both parents share in the responsibilities of raising of their children

legal custody—a determination of who will make major decisions regarding a child's education, medical care, and religious training; the two main types are joint custody and sole custody

legal separation—a court decree that may address such
issues as division of some assets, debts, and child support
and custody, while a couple is living separately

mediation—a process whereby a neutral person, called a
mediator, helps a divorcing couple solve their disputes by
mutual agreement

noncustodial parent—the parent whom the child does not
live with after a divorce and who may have visitation rights

parenting plan—a written agreement filed with the court
that outlines how parents will support and take care of their
children

physical custody—a determination of whom a child will live
with; the two main types are joint physical custody or sole
physical custody

sole custody—the parent or guardian with full responsibility for
the care of a child

therapist—a licensed mental health professional trained to help
people work through their behavioral issues; also may be
called a counselor

visitation—the legal right of the noncustodial parent to spend
time with his or her child

Books

Aydt, Rachel. *Why Me? A Teen Guide to Divorce and Your Feelings*. New York: The Rosen Publishing Group, 2000.

Calhoun, Florence. *No Easy Answers: A Teen's Guide to Why Divorce Happens*. New York: The Rosen Publishing Group, 2000.

Isler, Claudia. *Caught in the Middle: A Teen Guide to Custody*. New York: The Rosen Publishing Group, 2000.

Savage, Elayne. *Don't Take It Personally! The Art of Dealing with Rejection*. Lincoln, Neb.: iUniverse, 2002.

Worthen, Tom, ed. *broken hearts … healing: young poets speak out on divorce*. Logan, Utah: Poet Tree Press, 2001.

Videos

Dear Distant Dad: The Story of Lonely, Hurting Teens and Their Dads. Worcester, Pa.: Gateway Films/Vision Video, 1992.

When Mom and Dad Divorce. Niles, Ill.: United Learning Incorporated, 1994.

Online Sites & Organizations

Crisis Services
Kids Helpline
2969 Main Street
Buffalo, NY 14214
877/KIDS-400
www.kidscrisis.com

At this Web site, you can learn more about divorce, depression, eating disorders, and self-esteem issues. Join a chat room, read the Kids Helpline newsletter, or register for live chats. If you are having trouble and need to talk to a counselor now, the toll-free Helpline is open 24 hours a day.

Kids 4 Kids
www.kids4kids.com

Founded by Daniela Romano, a child of divorce, and her dad, this Web site offers teenagers a safe place to freely express their feelings regarding divorce, discuss problems, offer support, and find hope.

Kids in the Middle, Inc.
121 West Monroe
St. Louis, MO 63122
www.kidsinthemiddle.org

Log on to this site to read what other teens are saying about how divorce has impacted them and how they handle it. Read the Children's Bill of Rights, or explore other sections for tips on coping and setting boundaries.

Kids' Turn
1242 Market Street, 2nd Floor
San Francisco, CA 94102-4802
800/392-9239
www.kidsturn.org

A nonprofit organization helping kids and their families work through divorce, Kids' Turn has a Web site that features activities, artwork, articles, and frequently asked questions regarding divorce. Get advice from professionals and other teens on how to talk to your parents about divorce.

S

sadness, 11, 12, 32, 49, 66, 67, 75, 81
"Sam," 77
Savage, Elayne, 24, 33, 83
school counselors, 13, 76, 91
second marriages, 8, 10, 27
self-esteem, 78, 81, 83, 102
self-expression, 18, 66, 86, 99
separation, 25, 41, 44, 45, 47
shock, 11, 28
"silent treatment," 22
single-parent homes, 19
social workers, 15
sole custody, 53, 56
spousal support. *See* alimony.
spying, 35, 36
statistics
    arguments and divorce, 12
    attitude during divorce, 9
    child support, 48
    custodial parents, 58
    divorce rate, 8, 11, 16, 43
    divorce rate by state, 46
    mediation, 51
    odds of divorce, 10
    post-divorce adjustment, 102
    regrets about divorce, 69
    visitations, 82
    wedding anniversaries, 23
"Stephanie," 97
stepparents, 96
stomachaches, 87
stress, 18, 24, 42, 64, 85, 87
substance abuse, 9, 10, 14, 24, 72
support groups, 95
support systems, 18, 55, 64, 91, 92–93, 99
support system quiz, 92–93
Sweden, 26

T

"taking sides," 35, 36, 50
talking. *See* communication.
teachers, 13, 55, 67, 91
therapists, 15, 66, 75, 92
therapy, 92, 93
"Tori," 70
"Trevor," 28
Turkey, 26

U

U.S. Census Bureau, 10, 16, 23, 27, 43, 48
U.S. Department of Agriculture (USDA), 88, 90
United Kingdom, 26

V

verbal abuse, 10, 22, 24, 25
visitations, 35, 49, 53, 56, 57, 58, 61, 79, 82

W

Wade, Dwyane, 19
warning signs, 22
Web sites
    Divorce Forum, 8, 9
    Divorce Magazine, 9, 25, 33, 67, 69
    Kids 4 Kids network, 94–95
    MyPyramid program, 90
"Will," 71
Within a Child's Heart (Craig Henry Leibel), 103
worry, 13, 35, 55
Wyoming, 46

About the Author

Trudi Strain Trueit is an award-winning health and medical broadcast journalist. A news reporter for KREM-TV (CBS) in Spokane, Washington, her weekly on-air segment, "Your Health", earned recognition from the Society of Professional Journalists. She hosted *Unborn Ethics*, a documentary examining the controversy over genetic engineering, which received top national honors from United Press International. She is also a former television weather forecaster.

Ms. Trueit's other health titles for Franklin Watts include *Eating Disorders, ADHD, Sleep & Dreams*, and *Keeping a Journal*. In addition, she has written more than forty fiction and nonfiction books for children. She has a bachelor's degree in broadcast journalism and makes her home north of Seattle, Washington, with her husband, Bill.